# TOEFL

# ESSAY

# COLLECTION

# with

# WORKSPACE

# Table of Contents

SAMPLE ESSAY ONE ....................................................................................4

EXERCISE ONE .........................................................................................6

SAMPLE ESSAY TWO ...............................................................................10

EXERCISE TWO .......................................................................................12

SAMPLE ESSAY THREE ...........................................................................16

EXERCISE THREE ...................................................................................18

SAMPLE ESSAY FOUR ............................................................................22

EXERCISE FOUR ....................................................................................26

SAMPLE ESSAY FIVE ..............................................................................30

EXERCISE FIVE ......................................................................................33

SAMPLE ESSAY SIX .................................................................................37

EXERCISE SIX .........................................................................................40

SAMPLE ESSAY SEVEN ..........................................................................44

EXERCISE SEVEN ...................................................................................46

SAMPLE ESSAY EIGHT ...........................................................................50

EXERCISE EIGHT ...................................................................................52

SAMPLE ESSAY NINE .............................................................................56

EXERCISE NINE ......................................................................................58

SAMPLE ESSAY TEN ..............................................................................62

EXERCISE TEN .......................................................................................67

SAMPLE ESSAY ELEVEN ........................................................................71

EXERCISE ELEVEN .................................................................................73

SAMPLE ESSAY TWELVE .......................................................................77

EXERCISE TWELVE ................................................................................79

SAMPLE ESSAY THIRTEEN ....................................................................83

EXERCISE THIRTEEN .............................................................................85

SAMPLE ESSAY FOURTEEN ...................................................................89

EXERCISE FOURTEEN ............................................................................91

SAMPLE ESSAY FIFTEEN .......................................................................95

EXERCISE FIFTENN ...............................................................................97

# SAMPLE ESSAY ONE

*Do you agree or disagree with the following statement? Face-to-face communication is better than other types of communication, such as letters, email, or telephone calls. Use specific reasons and details to support your answer.*

In today's fast-paced environment, we are faced with a myriad of communication options. Be it letters, e-mails, or telephonic conversations, I think that no means is more effective than face-to-face dialogue.

Firstly, face-to-face dialogue affords the speaker the opportunity to convey his message in a more detailed and complete way. Emotions, moods and expressions come forth to the surface in a face-to-face interaction, unlike written words or those spoken on the telephone. By using tone, facial gestures and body language, the speaker gives a thorough idea of the listener of his point of view. For example, by leaning forward on his chair, opening his arms and moving his hands in a forceful manner, the speaker can convey interest and leadership.

Another benefit that face-to-face communication provides is immediate feedback. The speaker can clarify any confusion right away. Unlike written statements, no idea or thought is lost in grammatical errors or misuse of vocabulary. Since all people involved in the conversation can easily see each other, approval, interest, or disregard, can easily be deduced and dealt with. Often we see messages getting confused, and warped up in a maze of paperwork or unanswered e-mail and telephone calls. Such accumulation of data can create lot of stress and undue mess-ups in an office environment. Renowned CEOs, like Bill Gates are famous for making a point to show up at all business meetings, and if not possible, designate another person instead of using written words, or the telephone.

They say, "Nothing can replace the human touch." When people say that, what they mean is that the openness, camaraderie, and opportunity for feedback obtained through face-to-face dialogue is totally irreplaceable and invaluable.

# EXERCISE ONE

**Nowadays, food has become easier to prepare. Has this change improved the way people live? Use specific reasons and examples to support your answer.**

_____

_____

_____

_____

_____

_____

_____

_____

_____

_____

_____

_____

**It has recently been announced that a new high school may be built in your community. Do you support or oppose this plan? Why? Use specific reasons and details in your answer.**

_____

_____

_____

_____

_____

_____

_____

_____

_____

_____

_____

_____

# SAMPLE ESSAY TWO

**It has been said, "Not everything that is learned is contained in books." Compare and contrast knowledge gained from experience with knowledge gained from books. In your opinion, which source is more important? Why?**

People are always learning and practicing through their whole lives. From reading words in textbook such as toy, car, train etc., people have the concept and ideas. They further understand the actual meaning of these words by playing toys and riding or driving cars, trains etc. Education (books) and experience are the main two channels for People to gain their knowledge. Each plays different roles for people. In my opinion, knowledge from experience is more important than that from books.

Experience first can prove if the knowledge formbooks are true or false. Textbooks are very wonderful in teaching people essential principles, how is the world looks like? What is the basic law of change of people and things? We can learn a lot through primary school, secondary school until university. However, people can only understand the really meaning of those form books and justify them if they are right through practices. A few hundred years ago, people learnt from textbook that the earth was flat.

However scientists found that was wrong through observations and measurement.

The knowledge from experience can improve and advance The world and our society. As books have limitation, they only teach us what people found in the past. The knowledge from the books are constrained to the certain conditions and environment. For example, mould and tools design for plastics industry, the university course only taught me very simple cases, most knowledge is obtained from various different and complicated cases in my career. There are a lot new inventions and new products, which could not be found from textbooks. Our society and world are developed through continuous practices, those knowledge, never found in books, such as internet, e-business etc. are all developed through new practices.

"The truth comes from practices and experience", people are continually discovering new things and assessing the creditability of the knowledge written in books. The knowledge from experience helps us much more than those from books.

# EXERCISE TWO

**A company has announced that it wishes to build a large factory near your community. Discuss the advantages and disadvantages of this new influence on your community. Do you support or oppose the factory? Explain your position.**

_____

_____

_____

_____

_____

_____

_____

_____

_____

_____

_____

*Some people spend their entire lives in one place. Others move a number of times throughout their lives, looking for a better job, house, community, or even climate. Which do you prefer: staying in one place or moving in search of another place? Use reasons and specific examples to support your opinion.*

_____

_____

_____

_____

_____

_____

_____

_____

_____

_____

_____

# SAMPLE ESSAY THREE

**If you could change one important thing about your hometown, what would you change? Use reasons and specific examples to support your answer.**

Everything in the universe is in constant change. And everything needs continual improvement if the ever changing and increasing demands of humankind are to be met. If I were ever given the chance to change one important thing about my hometown, it would be Internet service. Needless to say that nothing generally revolutionized the way we live as Internet in the past decade. Thus, an improvement in this vital service would mean an even more, unheard betterment to the people in my hometown.

It is said that information is power. True saying indeed! I can envision how everything in my hometown could improve dramatically if the Internet service in it were made free, fast and staying out there like electricity, telephone or water all the time. One thing, a fast free and reliable Internet service could improve in my hometown is the way people work. If there is this said service people in my hometown must not necessarily commute to a far place to do their job. This in turn would mean less traffic jams, spacious work place, more time for family and recreation and so on.

The way people learn would be another important thing that a fast, free and reliable Internet service could better in my hometown. People will have the chance to go through tremendous and different information resources in a very small amount of time. They apparently will also take less time to share it. This assures a more fulfilled life for my hometown people. Since its advent, Internet touched every part of our life. It in a dazzling way improved the way we do business, learn and communicate. A change in Internet service implies good way of living for everyone in my hometown.

# EXERCISE THREE

**How do movies or television influence people's behavior? Use reasons and specific examples to support your answer.**

_____

_____

_____

_____

_____

_____

_____

_____

_____

_____

_____

_____

*Is it better to enjoy your money when you earn it or is it better to save your money for some time in the future? Use specific reasons and examples to support your opinion.*

_____

_____

_____

_____

_____

_____

_____

_____

_____

_____

_____

_____

# SAMPLE ESSAY FOUR

**Do you agree or disagree with the following statement? Television has destroyed communication among friends and family. Use specific reasons and examples to support your opinion.**

Television is undoubtedly one of the most powerful means of communication in the history of humankind, rivaled only by such other forms of communication as the Internet, the telephone, movies, and, of course, simple, low-tech speech. Television, with its wide availability and rich media with image and sound, is difficult to ignore and even seductive in its appeal. Television is as much a part of our lives as are our meals, work, or school; studies consistently show that the average American child spends almost as much time watching television as she does in school. Furthermore, because television is so rich in its media, it often requires our full attention or is more attraction to us than are our daily lives. Naturally, the more time one spends watching television, the less time she has with her family and friends. Thus, we can clearly see why some have claimed that television has been harmful for communication among family and friends. However, I believe that, while television has been somewhat harmful in its effects, it has hardly "destroyed" communication among family and friends for most people, although for some, this may be true.

Most people much prefer spending time with their families and friends to spending time watching television. Television is of course an important part of many people's lives, but most people would gladly choose family and friends over television were they given the choice.

Furthermore, most educated people are aware of the deleterious effects of too much television and either avoid excessive time watching television, or actually do not enjoy it. I, for example, after a long day at work, would much rather spend time talking with my wife and playing with my children than I would watching some unrealistic portrayal of life on television. For my family, and me our time together is precious and beautiful, and could never be replaced or hurt by television.

Furthermore, the effect of television is simply not so great that it could be said to have "destroyed" communication among family and friends. Granting that communication among family and friends in industrialized countries has decreased in recent years, it might be tempting to blame this problem on television since its rise roughly coincided with the decrease in time we spend with our families. However, I believe this situation is more likely due to increased pressures relating from work, school, and the economy. In my case, for example, I find that my pressures from work are so great that I must often sacrifice time at home so that I can meet the challenges of running my own business. Many of my friends are in similar situations--my best friend, for example, has just finished law school, which took about sixty hours a week of his time. In a word, people nowadays have very little time for anything, but  television is not the cause--it is increased desire to succeed.

In some situations, however, television has surely contributed to a decrease in communication among family members. In my childhood in the countryside, I often saw parents and children watching television for hours on end, rarely speaking with one another. It seemed for them that television was a way to escape from their sad, miserable existence. However, even in this case, I would say that television merely contributed to the bad situation, but did not cause it; were television not existent, surely these people would have found other escapes, alcohol or gambling, for example. In other words, people always find a way to do what they want to do.

In short, I do not believe that television has destroyed or even harmed interpersonal communication among most people. Most people realize that television is merely a temporary diversion and do not use it to replace interpersonal communication. I believe that the damage attributed to television is greatly exaggerated and that such damage is most likely attributable to other more powerful social factors.

# EXERCISE FOUR

Some people prefer to live in a small town. Others prefer to live in a big city. Which place would you prefer to live in? Use specific reasons and details to support your answer.

_____

_____

_____

_____

_____

_____

_____

_____

_____

_____

_____

_____

_____

*You have received a gift of money. The money is enough to buy either a piece of jewelry you like or tickets to a concert you want to attend. Which would you buy? Use specific reasons and details to support your answer.*

_____

_____

_____

_____

_____

_____

_____

_____

_____

_____

_____

_____

_____

_____

# SAMPLE ESSAY FIVE

**"When people succeed, it is because of hard work. Luck has nothing to do with success." Do you agree or disagree with the quotation above? Use specific reasons and examples to explain your position.**

I fully agree with the claim that there is no correlation between success and luck. Moreover, I understand success to refer to one's ability to achieve the predominant part of his goals in his lifetime, which in turn leads to a correlation between success and income since the accomplishment of such a natural goal as to provide a good future for your loved ones demands the means. What is the simplest and most lawful way to earn enough to consider you a successful person? To receive a good education and to find a good job. Both receiving an education and making a career presuppose one's readiness to work hard, and success without hard work is simply not possible for the vast majority of the world's population. The reasons and examples listed below will strengthen my point of view.

First of all, considering an education and a career as key factors of success, one will choose to pursue a degree from a college or a university. One wishing to be admitted to the university will have to take several tests. It is doubtful that someone will be so lucky that knowing nothing; he could pass the test with a high score. A low score means failure, and that test taker will not likely be admitted. Therefore, in order to be successful, one should prepare for the tests and work hard, because a good education will provide him with a good job and an opportunity to accomplish some of his goals and dreams. In my lifetime, I have never met a person who could graduate from a college without working hard.

Secondly, it is impossible to make a career if one is indolent and lacking knowledge, at least in developed countries. Luck plays no role in achieving this success. Even if someone was unbelievably lucky enough to become a manager not being qualified enough, he will be asked to resign in the near future because of his inability due to lack of knowledge and experience to make right decisions. For instance, I used to work for a very small company owned by a friend. This company was later closed because of bankruptcy. The cause of bankruptcy was wrong strategies and decisions made by the owner. After the failure, he went to a university and worked for another company so that he could obtain experience and become a successful businessman. Nowadays, he considers himself a successful person because he had turned into reality his two biggest dreams of producing consumer goods of high quality and making charitable donations to needy people.

In sum, as long as someone understands success as an ability to turn into reality some of his dreams and goals, he will have to work hard because he will need money. And his chances to earn that money will remarkably increase if he could graduate from a college and make a career. All of these things are simply not possible without hard work. Luck has no place in such a scheme of events.

# EXERCISE FIVE

Do you agree or disagree with the following statement? Universities should give the same amount of money to their students' sports activities as they give to their university libraries. Use specific reasons and examples to support your opinion.

_____

_____

_____

_____

_____

_____

_____

_____

_____

_____

*Businesses should hire employees for their entire lives. Do you agree or disagree? Use specific reasons and examples to support your answer.*

_____

_____

_____

_____

_____

_____

_____

_____

_____

_____

_____

_____

_____

# SAMPLE ESSAY SIX

**Some people prefer to eat at food stands or restaurants. Other people prefer to prepare and eat food at home. Which do you prefer? Use specific reasons and examples to support your answer.**

People may have two choices to eat, either they go out to fast food stands or restaurants, or they prepare food at home, whatever suitable to them. In my case I prefer to go out to eat, as it is easy to get, it saves my time, and I can try variety of interesting food of different countries. Being a working person, with all day long office work and driving long way, it becomes difficult to do all preparation for making food.

For me easy way to get food is restaurant, where I can get prepared food at home or office by just ordering on phone, Along with that another comfort is, that when ever I have to eat together with my so many friends, I can always go to a restaurant, otherwise it's difficult to prepare food at home for so many people and don't get time to talk and having fun. So I always find it a easier way to eat out, apart from that It make my other outdoor activities possible because I don't have to bother about food wherever I go, to any fun place or theater or traveling, restaurants are always there throughout city and it becomes easy every time to get food whenever and whenever I need according to other activities.

Besides that I can save a lot of time by getting food from restaurant as, I don't have to go for vegetables and grocery shopping, I don't need to clean, cut and fry food and do a lot kitchen work, doing dishes etc., instead I can get fresh food delivered in minutes. Along with that when I eat at restaurant I have more time to do other things like reading, watching TV, and listening music, going out theatre, or having fun with friends, that don't make me tired or boring and I feel refreshed for next day work, so by going to restaurant I can manage a lot more activities instead preparing food.

In addition, in restaurant I get a variety of food choice, I can have taste of different regions, for example Indian restaurant I can get varied food from North Indian to South Indian Punjabi, Bengali, Madrasi, Maharashtrian, etc. at one place. Likewise, I can taste world wide food variety like pasta dishes in Italian restaurant, tortilla and burrito dishes in Mexican, pizza, and burger items in American, noodles in Chinese, etc. and can enjoy various vegetarian, non-vegetarian dishes which are specialty of different countries.

Not only that, in restaurant the food is served with beautiful garnishing, that tempts for eating and is worth of paying. I find it very interesting to experience varied food in different restaurants.

To conclude I am fond of going stands and restaurants for eating that is suitable for me because of convenient, quick and variety of tasty food, which I enjoy very much and make my routine easier and interesting.

# EXERCISE SIX

*Some people believe that university students should be required to attend classes. Others believe that going to classes should be optional for students. Which point of view do you agree with? Use specific reasons and details to explain your answer.*

_____

_____

_____

_____

_____

_____

_____

_____

_____

_____

_____

_____

*Do you agree or disagree with the following statement? Attending a live performance (for example, a play, concert, or sporting event) is more enjoyable than watching the same event on television. Use specific reasons and examples to support your opinion.*

_____

_____

_____

_____

_____

_____

_____

_____

_____

_____

_____

_____

_____

# SAMPLE ESSAY SEVEN

*Neighbors are the people who live near us. In your opinion, what are the qualities of a good neighbor? Use specific details and examples in your answer.*

Neighbors are part of our daily lives. They are part of the process of socialization. Socialization is the process in which we interact with other people. In our lives we are always trying to look for a good area to live, a nice house, and most important of all good neighbors. This will influence in the decision of either moving to the area, or star looking for another area. In my opinion a good neighbor will be those who are respectful, friendly, and helpful

The first quality that good neighbors should have is to be respectful. Respect is the most important aspect of being good neighbor. Neighbors should respect your space and privacy in order to live in a peaceful environment. Being a respectful neighbor means not invading your personal space as well as your property. Another example will be to maintain a quiet environment not allowing loud music, or noise that will bother others.          Respect          to          one another is the most important quality that a neighbor should have in order to live in harmony.

Another quality of a good neighbor is that it should be friendly. All people should be friendly to one another, but this quality is most important when it comes to neighbors. Neighbors are close to you, to your home, property and most important to your family. You might not see them every day, but they live next to you all the time. These are the reasons why they should be friendly. One of the ways to be friendly is by showing they care about you, and they should welcome you to their neighborhood. Friendly neighbors

make a good and united society. The last quality of good neighbor is that it should be helpful. Neighbors as well as everyone should be helpful to one another. Helpfulness is a characteristic that everyone should have. A helpful neighbor is that, that in the times of need is there for you. For example, if a person is in a situation where he/she needs a moral support for the lost a loving family member, the neighbor should give this person all the support he/she might need and encourage he/she that they can count on them no matter what.

Overall good neighbors are those whom are respectful in every way. Friendly, that every time you see them they greet you with a good smile. And good neighbors are those whom are helpful when ever you need a supporting hand.

# EXERCISE SEVEN

It has recently been announced that a new restaurant may be built in your neighborhood. Do you support or oppose this plan? Why? Use specific reasons and details to support your answer.

---

---

---

---

---

---

---

---

---

---

*Choose one of the following transportation vehicles and explain why you think it has changed people's lives. • Automobiles • Bicycles • Airplanes*

_____

_____

_____

_____

_____

_____

_____

_____

_____

_____

_____

_____

# SAMPLE ESSAY EIGHT

**Some people think that they can learn better by themselves than with a teacher. Others think that it is always better to have a teacher. Which do you prefer? Use specific reasons to develop your essay**

I support the view that teachers should be a part of the learning process. Below are several beneficial reasons for which I feel that teachers are needed in while learning. Below are also some of the problems that come up without their presence.

Primarily teachers are there for guidance in a particular field or subject. They give you a systematic and better way to approach a subject. A teacher normally teaches a subject in which he or she has expertise. Hence that person has made a study of the subject and can guide you in order to help you approach the subject in a better way. This guidance may be in the form of giving you names of reference books or giving you notes. Without a teacher it would be extremely cumbersome to go through large libraries for a certain topic. Besides this the teacher could provide you help with any sort of problem that you come across while studying. The teacher could provide you strategies that help you solve a problem. Without a teacher, this problem would take up a lot of your                   valuable                   time                   or remain unsolved. Teachers can also point out when you are going wrong. They point out our mistakes and suggest ways for us to correct them.

In the end it does depend on the individual person to finally getting down to learn a subject. The actual studying has to be done by the individual. But the learning process can be made much simpler with the proper and continuous guidance of teachers. Hence it betters to learn with the help of a teacher rather than learning by you.

# EXERCISE EIGHT

**What are some important qualities of a good supervisor (boss)? Use specific details and examples to explain why these qualities are important.**

_____

_____

_____

_____

_____

_____

_____

_____

_____

_____

_____

_____

_____

*Do you agree or disagree that progress is always good? Use specific reasons and examples to support your answer.*

_____

_____

_____

_____

_____

_____

_____

_____

_____

_____

_____

_____

_____

# SAMPLE ESSAY NINE

*Should governments spend more money on improving roads and highways, or should governments spend more money on improving public transportation (buses, trains, and subways)? Why? Use specific reasons and details to develop your essay.*

All means of transportation should be kept in good conditions. However, I believe it would be most beneficial for a country or city, if its government spent more money on improving public transportation. This would result in substantial standard of living improvements.

The volume of cars and trucks hitting the highways is dramatically rising every year. As a result, the number of traffic jams, accidents and carbon monoxide emissions are doing too. All these factors have a detrimental effect on our quality of life. Expanding subway lines and railroads and developing an effective plan to combine buses and subways routes, would eventually lead to a reduction in pollution levels, less traffic jams and less stress for the people.

If subway lines reached every corner of a city, people would not need to use their cars to commute. Less cars on the road, means less carbon monoxide emissions into the atmosphere; therefore, the air we breathe would be more pure. Less cars also means less traffic jams, which translates into less stress for drivers and better living conditions.

Not every country has a well-developed railroad system. Consequently, they have to rely on trucks and buses for ground transportation of passengers and freight. Expanding and upgrading railroad systems will result in fewer trucks and buses on the highways. Removing this kind of traffic from the highways and encouraging the use of trains, would be another way to reduce congestion on the freeways. The reduction of traffic represents less maintenance costs for the government. This surplus of money could be use for other purposes. For example, a forest recovery program or a national campaign against pollution.

Highways, roads and public transportation all require maintenance funds, but I think it is more important to think about the future and how to make our countries or cities better places to live in. Improving public transportation will help reduce traffic jams, accidents and air pollution. A safer, healthier and more enjoyable place to live waits for us in the future.

# EXERCISE NINE

*It is better for children to grow up in the countryside than in a big city. Do you agree or disagree? Use specific reasons and examples to develop your essay.*

_____

_____

_____

_____

_____

_____

_____

_____

_____

_____

_____

_____

*Learning about the past has no value for those of us living in the present. Do you agree or disagree? Use specific reasons and examples to support your answer.*

_____

_____

_____

_____

_____

_____

_____

_____

_____

_____

_____

_____

_____

_____

# SAMPLE ESSAY TEN

*In general, people are living longer now. Discuss the causes of this phenomenon. Use specific reasons and details to develop your essay.*

A greater number of people are now hitting the eighty-year mark than ten years ago. In fact, the life expectancy of the average human has gone up considerably, and is rising still. This phenomenon is the result of several reasons. For one, continuing scientific                                                                 and medical innovation ensure that more people receive the treatment they require. As our knowledge grows regarding various diseases, we become better equipped to tackle them. Consequently, we have managed to eradicate some diseases on a global scale, while controlling the other diseases, so that the rate of mortality does not reach an alarming height during the outbreak of a disease. The plagues of yore, as well as the more recent plague outbreaks are becoming few and far in between. Such control of diseases means that the general life expectancy has gone up.

Diseases such as cancer, which used to result almost inevitably in death, are now curable, provided they are diagnosed at a certain stage. Diseases such as tuberculosis and cholera now cause fewer deaths than they used to only a few decades ago. Another reason for the greater life expectancy is the general betterment of the quality of life. What we call the 'global village' is fast becoming a city. And in this city, more and more people are being provided a better level of hygiene than ever before. A better and improving system of communication ensures that the latest medical discoveries in the United States and Europe are known all over the world in a space of a few days. Therefore, more and more people have access to better health care. Even people living in relatively

remote areas have access to some kind of medical facilities. Though these facilities may be incapable of handling a crisis, they may help prevent death in cases that require antibiotics and antivenin, thereby preventing death by infection or poison.

The increase in awareness also means that people in general are becoming more aware of the risks of various diseases. For instance, more people now, than two decades ago, are aware of the scourge of cholesterol and the havoc it wreaks on an individual's                                        circulatory system. Similarly people are becoming aware that prevention is, after all, better than cure and are taking the appropriate steps to prevent infection from diseases. In general, though, the increased life expectancy owes much to the revolution in communication. It may be mentioned that even two hundred years ago, inventions and discoveries were being made. However, they did few people any good. It simply took too long to disseminate the information. The general level of awareness regarding health was also low. However, it has been noticed that since the inception of communication through first print, and then radio and television, the level of awareness regarding health has generally risen. To illustrate, print facilitated the spread of knowledge through books. Radio helped bring that knowledge to many people. Television helped to further this knowledge and disseminate is amongst an even greater number of people.

And finally, the Internet has removed the final barriers between intercultural and interracial communication. In the coming years, we may hope to see an even greater increase in life expectancy, even as communication techniques continue to improve.

**ANSWER B**

According to the latest statistics, the average life span of human beings is about 75-79 years old. Comparing to that ten years ago, it has been increased by 10%. Advancement in technology, better lifestyle and nutritional diets are the main reasons for prolonged lives.

Advancement in technology helps to bring about new methods of curing fatal diseases. Cancer used to have no cure in the last decade, but recently new methods such as X-ray treatment and various types of injections are introduced which can greatly extend                                                     the patients' lives. Advancement in technology also improves the quality of medical instruments. This lowers the risk and minimizes the possible side effects of various operations.

People nowadays are having better lifestyle than in the past. They are more aware of the importance of healthiness. Compulsory annual body checks help to prevent the condition to worsen and the spread of diseases. People become more depending on their family doctors when they are sick instead of consuming medicine that is not given by their doctors. They also learn to maintain a suitable amount of workload and take breaks in order to be healthy psychologically. This can minimize the chances of getting the diseases that are stress related such as heart attack.

Balanced diet is not only a motto for people who are keeping fit, but also applies to the general public. People become more aware of the choice of food. They start to pay attention to the nutritional values of food. This can serve as a guideline to prevent people from overeating certain types of food and ignoring the nutritional food. It can therefore improve the healthiness of the public as a whole. It can also reduce the chances for malnutrition and can help extend the life span of human beings.

To conclude, advancement in technology and raising awareness in healthy lifestyle help to extend the life span of human beings. We can predict that in the future, people can live longer and healthier, and more methods of curing diseases will be introduced.

# EXERCISE TEN

*We all work or will work in our jobs with many different kinds of people. In your opinion, what are some important characteristics of a co-worker (someone you work closely with)? Use reasons and specific examples to explain why these characteristics*
*are important.*

_____

_____

_____

_____

_____

_____

_____

_____

_____

_____

_____

_____

*Do you agree or disagree with the following statement? With the help of technology, students nowadays can learn more information and learn it more quickly. Use specific reasons and examples to support your answer.*

_____

_____

_____

_____

_____

_____

_____

_____

_____

_____

---

---

# SAMPLE ESSAY ELEVEN

*In some countries, teenagers have jobs while they are still students. Do you think this is a good idea? Support your opinion by using specific reasons and details.*

Nowadays, a lot of teens work in jobs while they are studying. Some of them really need the money they earn to compensate for their school expenses whereas others use the money they earn as pocket money. Whatever the reason for the students to work in jobs is, in my opinion, working is a great experience to all. Having a job is an important opportunity to learn about responsibilities and also teaches the teenagers to cooperate with their co-workers and enable them to understand the value of money.

To start with, working in a job gives teenagers lots of situations in which they should act responsibly; otherwise they will lose their jobs. For example, one has to wake up early if his/her working hours start at 8:00 AM in the morning, no matter how late he/she stayed up last night. Otherwise, his/her supervisor will warn him/her or may eventually fire the individual. A second reason why having jobs as students has positive effects on teenagers is that                                        it teaches them how to cooperate and the importance of cooperation. In a work setting usually the employees have to depend on each other on numerous occasions. When a single employee loafs, others will have to compensate for his/her workload in addition to their own tasks. Students will learn from their working experience the importance of cooperation and why every individual should effectively carry out his/her own work.

Another point is, these working possibilities enable the students to understand the value of money and that "Money does not grow on trees". After the student sees how hard he/she has to work to earn money, he/she will also be more reasonable while spending it, thus, his/her purchasing behavior will be enhanced.

In conclusion, when one has a job as a student, he/she will benefit significantly from the experience. This way, students will be more responsible when they graduate. Furthermore, they will be more cooperative, thus will be more beneficial for the companies they will be working in once they will be graduated. Finally, since they'll know better how to spend their money, they won't get into trouble due to excessive spending. All in all, having jobs as students is a terrific idea and I think every student should have a working experience before graduating and starting their professional careers.

## EXERCISE ELEVEN

*A person you know is planning to move to your town or city. What do you think this person would like and dislike about living in your town or city? Why? Use specific reasons and details to develop your essay.*

_____

_____

_____

_____

_____

_____

_____

_____

_____

_____

_____

_____

*The expression "Never, never give up" means to keep trying and never stop working for your goals. Do you agree or disagree with this statement? Use specific reasons and examples to support your answer.*

_____

_____

_____

_____

_____

_____

_____

_____

_____

_____

_____

_____

## SAMPLE ESSAY TWELVE

*It has recently been announced that a large shopping center may be built in your neighborhood. Do you support or oppose this plan? Why? Use specific reasons and details to support your answer.*

My hometown, Pentair Remiss, is a small fishing village located in west Malaysia. You can hardly find a shopping center there in the neighborhood. I, together with most of the residents in this town, would definitely most welcome the proposal of building a large

shopping center in our neighborhood. Nearly one half of the residents in my neighborhood have to seek for a job in big city like

Kuala Lumpur or Singapore. This is because most of the youngsters in my village are reluctant to follow their ancestors' step to become a fisherman. They wish to pursue a better job in the city. By building a big shopping center, it will surely bring up a lot of working opportunities for the community. Some can work as executives while others can work as salesperson in the shopping center.

Other than that, the establishment of a large shopping center will provide the community a more comfortable and more convenient place to shop. As the weather in Malaysia is so hot, it will be an ideal spot to go shopping for its air-conditioning environment compared to the small stuffy grocery store down the town. On the other hand, it is much more convenient to shop in large shopping center where you can get nearly most of the goods here, from veggies to undergarments, just name it.

Furthermore, the shopping center will most probably benefit the community by offering goods in better price. The shopping center will eventually exist as a main competitor to the other grocery stores and sundry shops in town. Therefore, every store will try to win their customers by lowering the price and at the same time offering better services. And the customer will certainly be the winner in this 'pricing war'.

In a conclusion, I fully advocate the idea of building a big shopping center in my neighborhood, which will be beneficial to this small town.

# EXERCISE TWELVE

*It has recently been announced that a new movie theater may be built in your neighborhood. Do you support or oppose this plan? Why? Use specific reasons and details to support your answer.*

_____

_____

_____

_____

_____

_____

_____

_____

_____

_____

_____

_____

*Some people think that human needs for farmland, housing, and industry are more important than saving land for endangered animals. Do you agree or disagree with this point of view? Why or why not? Use specific reasons and examples to support your answer.*

_____

_____

_____

_____

_____

_____

_____

_____

_____

_____

_____

# SAMPLE ESSAY THIRTEEN

*Do you agree or disagree with the following statement? People should sometimes do things that they do not enjoy doing. Use specific reasons and examples to support your answer.*

I do agree with the statement that people should sometimes do things that they don't enjoy doing. And I would rather go as far as saying that they should try to enjoy things they are forced to do.

To exemplify, consider the following situations. Not all children love to study. Instead, being curious and enthusiastic, they love to explore the world around them, paying less attention to studies and more to other things. Should they be allowed to give up their studies? Certainly not. Or consider a very talented person, say a person with great academic record and excellent analytical skills trying for a job. Suppose the person is introvert but the company's recruitment process demands that he should go in through a group discussion. Should he give up because of this? I would strongly oppose his decision, if he does. Or consider a sportsperson being forced to go in for a drug test, because rules demand him to do so. The person being from a conservative background feels uncomfortable with this. Should he give up the sport just because he is being forced to do something he doesn't like? Well, I would say no.

So, the point is that there are situations in life, when one has to do something he/she doesn't like. And not doing the thing may have a large impact on his life. So, it's sometimes wise to go against one's wishes. I don't advocate that one should always go against one's wishes when he/she is forced to take such decisions. It depends upon the importance and the urgency of a situation. For instance, one might want to quit up a job that one doesn't like. He may, infect he should do so, for perpetually doing something one doesn't like makes one's life miserable. But what if there's a recession in the economy and its hard to find jobs? He, of course should be careful in his decision, and it won't be unwise if he continues with his same, probably boring job.

To conclude, I would say that one should judge a situation according to its merits and make a wise decision whether or not he/she wants to do something, which he/she doesn't like. Compromising once in a while is sometimes a better choice.

# EXERCISE THIRTEEN

*Do you agree or disagree with the following statement?*
*Television, newspapers, magazines, and other media pay too*
*much attention to the personal lives of famous people such as*
*public figures and celebrities. Use specific reasons and details to*
*explain your opinion*

_____

_____

_____

_____

_____

_____

_____

_____

_____

_____

*Some people believe that the Earth is being harmed (damaged) by human activity. Others feel that human activity makes the Earth a better place to live. What is your opinion? Use specific reasons and examples to support your answer.*

_____

_____

_____

_____

_____

_____

_____

_____

_____

_____

_____

_____

_____

# SAMPLE ESSAY FOURTEEN

*What is a very important skill a person should learn in order to be successful in the world today? Choose one skill and use specific reasons and examples to support your choice.*

In my opinion an important skill that a person should learn in order to be successful in today's world is to keep him updated in every field.

It is said that knowledge is power. Keeping oneself updated in this high speed, changing world is very important. Knowledge is like a small drop in this vast ocean and there is no end for it. The more knowledge you gain, the more you need.

One of the advantages of keeping oneself aware is that nobody can mislead you in anyway. For example if you know the price of a car, you want to buy, would help you negotiate more rather than just agree to the dealers price. Keeping ourselves updated also boosts our confidence and also keeps us ahead in this competitive world.

We should develop this skill by listening to news, reading articles, learning new technologies. In short we should always keep on increasing our knowledge. If we do this then rest of the thing like wealth, fame, comforts will automatically come to us. Hence keeping yourself updated is very important skill everybody should acquire in today's world.

# EXERCISE FOURTEEN

*Why do you think some people are attracted to dangerous sports or other dangerous activities? Use specific reasons and examples to support your answer.*

_____

_____

_____

_____

_____

_____

_____

_____

_____

_____

_____

_____

_____

*Some people like to travel with a companion. Other people prefer to travel alone. Which do you prefer? Use specific reasons and examples to support your choice.*

_____

_____

_____

_____

_____

_____

_____

_____

_____

_____

_____

_____

# SAMPLE ESSAY FIFTEEN

*Some people prefer to get up early in the morning and start the day's work. Others prefer to get up later in the day and work until late at night. Which do you prefer? Use specific reasons and examples to support your choice.*

I prefer to get up early in the morning and start the day's work. First of all, my parents have helped me to develop the habit of getting up early in the morning since I was a kid. And I see this is a good habit because by getting up early, I have more hours in a day                                    to finish the day's work. For example, when I get up early in the morning, I would reach the office earlier. Normally, I would either have more time to finish the work or finish the work earlier and leave home earlier.

Another reason that I prefer to get up early is because I can enjoy the beauty of the nature. When I get up early, I can really feel the cool weather and fresh air in the morning. And I would say it is best time of the day to plan for the day's work.

I also choice to get up early because I can beat the traffic jam at my residential area. In most cases, I can avoid the hectic traffics and reach my office on time by getting up early in the morning.

By being in the office early, I show my commitment in my work and

become more productive.

In short, I prefer to get up early and start the day's work early because it allows me to have more hours to work per day. Also, I can plan well in the cool and fresh environment. Last but not least, getting up early also means I can beat the traffic jam and be more productive in my work.

# EXERCISE FIFTENN

*What are the important qualities of a good son or daughter? Have these qualities changed or remained the same over time in your culture? Use specific reasons and examples to support your answer.*

_____

_____

_____

_____

_____

_____

_____

_____

_____

_____

*Some people prefer to work for a large company. Others prefer to work for a small company. Which would you prefer? Use specific reasons and details to support your choice.*

Made in United States
Troutdale, OR
10/18/2024

23816273R00060